Guess-Me Poems & Puzzles: Word Families

by Betsy Franco

SCHOLASTIC
PROFESSIONAL BOOKS

New York ✫ Toronto ✫ London ✫ Auckland ✫ Sydney
Mexico City ✫ New Delhi ✫ Hong Kong ✫ Buenos Aires

For Young kuk Lee,
who helps me with my books

Cover design by Gerard Fuchs

Cover and interior illustrations by Rusty Fletcher

Interior design by Ellen Matlach Hassell
for Boultinghouse & Boultinghouse

ISBN: 0-439-38773-6

Copyright © 2003 by Betsy Franco.

All rights reserved.

Printed in the U.S.A.

3 4 5 6 7 8 9 10 40 09 08 07 06 05 04 03

Contents

The Mini-Books

Introduction

We thoroughly delight the children in your class.
We teach phonemic awareness and spelling skills.
We build reading skills.
Who are we?

The answer to this riddle is: *Guess-Me Poems & Puzzles!* In this book, you will find twenty-five adorable, easy-to-make pocket puzzles, one for each of the top 25 word families. They're designed for introducing, building, reinforcing, and practicing word families There are a number of ways these puzzles can be used:

- Give each child his or her own mini-book and puzzle to make.
- Give one book to a pair of children to make and solve together.
- Have children take the pages home and complete with families.
- Create the books and puzzles yourself, laminate, and place in a learning center.

The puzzles are easily adapted for use with both younger and older children. With younger children, you can read the riddle to the class, then everyone can recite it with you. The activities can be completed together. After solving the puzzle, children can color in the illustration for fun.

With older children, the riddle can be read independently. Each child can work on the riddle, puzzle, and word bank on his or her own. The whole class can meet later to compile a master word bank and review the results. Puzzles can be colored in for fun.

In Each Mini-Book

- The first page of each packet presents a challenge, such as: "What Is the *–ack* Word?"
- The second page is a fun-filled riddle that children can solve. Each riddle contains additional words with the target word.
- The third page holds a jigsaw puzzle with the riddle's answer, both written and illustrated, and a line on which children write the answer.

- The last page leaves space for recording more words in the featured word family.

Making the Mini-Books and Puzzles

It will be helpful to first demonstrate each step to children.

1. Make a double-sided copy of the page.

2. Cut along the lines with the scissor icon. Put the puzzle pieces aside.

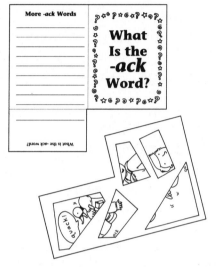

3. Fold up the flap and tape either side to the edges of the book so that it becomes a pouch.

4. Fold the book in half along the dotted line.

5. Cut out the puzzle pieces along the gray lines and put them in the pouch.

☆ ⓖ TIPS ☆ ⊙

- As younger children construct the puzzles, show them how to find the corners of the puzzle.

- When children are filling in the word banks, use the master word banks on pages 9–14 as a resource.

Activities

The following are fun, helpful, enriching activities you can do during or after the completion of the mini-book and puzzle:

☆ Have children highlight or underline the key words on their riddle page or a chart paper copy of the riddle. Or, copy the riddle onto pocket chart strips and have children point to the key words.

> The squirrels <u>yap</u>.
> The chipmunks <u>clap</u>.
> The turtles <u>snap</u>.
> The woodpeckers <u>tap</u>.
> They wake the bear up from his __ap!   (ANSWER: nap)

☆ For each word family, make a master list of all the rhyming words your children can think of. Alternatively, list the words on webs.

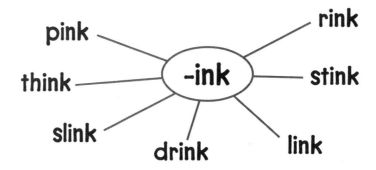

☆ Create word chains such as the one below, using words from the word banks. Then read each statement aloud and have children write the word you're describing.

> 1. Start with the word *pin*.
> 2. Switch the *n* and the *p* to make *nip*.
> 3. Add one letter to make *snip*.
> 4. Change one letter to make *skip*.
> 5. Take off one letter to make *sip*.
> 6. Change one letter to make *rip*.
> 7. Add one letter to make *trip*.

☆ If you have sets of letters for children to use, individually or in a learning center, let them create as many words as they can within a word family. Have them insert the rime (such as *-ack*) in the letter "rack" and try different beginning consonants. They can record the words they find.

☆ After children have read the complete riddle once, leave out the key words in the riddle and distribute a copy to each child. Have children fill in the missing words.

_____'s father _____
is a very helpful _____.
He drives on our field trips
whenever he _____.
Twelve children can fit
in his super-size _____!

☆ Have children alphabetize the words in the word bank.

bill
dill
fill
gill
hill
Jill
mill
pill
spill
still
will

☆ Write a new rhyming riddle about another word in the word family.

> On the classroom wall,
> it goes tick-tock.
> It tells the time.
> It's called a ___ock.   (ANSWER: clock)

☆ Write a non-rhyming riddle using three clues. The answer can be one of the words in the word bank.

> This food is eaten in Japan.
> It's white.
> It tastes good with soy sauce on it.   (ANSWER: rice)

☆ Have a child act out different words in the word bank and let the class guess the word family.

☆ Create a class collaborative book in which each child chooses a word family, draws a picture of a word from the word family, and writes a sentence using the word.

Word Family Word Banks

-ack	-ail	-ake	-an	-ank
back	ail	bake	an	bank
hack		cake		Hank
Jack	bail	fake	ban	lank
lack	fail	Jake	can	rank
Mack	Gail	lake	Dan	sank
pack	hail	make	fan	tank
quack	jail	quake	man	yank
rack	mail	rake	pan	
sack	nail	sake	ran	blank
tack	pail	take	tan	clank
	quail	wake	van	crank
black	rail			drank
clack	sail	awake	bran	flank
crack	tail	brake	clan	Frank
knack	wail	drake	plan	plank
shack		flake	scan	prank
slack	e-mail	shake	span	spank
smack	flail	snake	Stan	thank
snack	frail	stake	than	
stack	snail			
track	trail			
whack				

-ap	-at	-ay	-eep	-ell
cap	at	bay	beep	bell
gap		day	deep	cell
lap	bat	gay	jeep	dell
map	cat	hay	keep	fell
nap	fat	jay	peep	jell
rap	hat	lay	seep	Nell
sap	mat	may	weep	sell
tap	pat	nay		tell
yap	rat	pay	cheep	well
	sat	ray	creep	yell
chap	tat	say	sheep	
clap	vat	way	sleep	dwell
flap			steep	shell
scrap	brat	clay	sweep	smell
slap	chat	fray		spell
snap	drat	gray		swell
strap	flat	okay		
trap	scat	play		
wrap	slat	pray		
	spat	slay		
	that	spray		
		stay		
		stray		
		sway		
		tray		

-est	-ice	-ide	-ill	-in
best	ice	bide	ill	in
jest		hide		
lest	dice	ride	bill	bin
nest	lice	side	dill	fin
pest	mice	tide	fill	kin
rest	nice	wide	gill	pin
test	rice		hill	tin
vest	vice	bride	Jill	win
west		decide	kill	
zest	Brice	glide	mill	chin
	price	pride	pill	grin
blest	slice	slide	quill	shin
chest	splice	snide	sill	skin
crest	thrice	stride	till	thin
quest	twice		will	twin
wrest				
			chill	
			drill	
			frill	
			grill	
			skill	
			spill	
			still	
			thrill	
			trill	
			twill	
			downhill	

-ine	-ing	-ink	-ip	-ock
dine	bing	ink	dip	dock
fine	ding		hip	hock
line	king	kink	Kip	knock
mine	ping	link	lip	lock
nine	ring	mink	nip	mock
pine	sing	pink	quip	rock
vine	wing	rink	rip	sock
	zing	sink	sip	tock
brine		wink	tip	
divine	bring		zip	block
shine	cling	blink		Brock
shrine	fling	brink	blip	clock
spine	sling	clink	chip	crock
swine	spring	drink	clip	flock
whine	sting	shrink	drip	frock
	string	slink	flip	shock
	swing	stink	grip	smock
	thing	think	ship	stock
	wring		skip	
			slip	
			snip	
			strip	
			trip	
			whip	

-op	-ot	-uck	-ug	-ump
bop	cot	buck	bug	bump
cop	dot	duck	dug	dump
hop	got	luck	hug	hump
mop	hot	muck	lug	jump
pop	jot	puck	lug	lump
sop	knot	suck	mug	pump
top	lot	tuck	pug	rump
	not		rug	sump
chop	pot	Chuck	tug	
crop	rot	cluck		chump
drop	tot	pluck	chug	clump
flop		stuck	drug	frump
plop	blot	struck	plug	grump
prop	clot	truck	shrug	plump
shop	plot		slug	slump
slop	shot		smug	stump
stop	slot		snug	thump
	spot		thug	trump
	trot			
			unplug	

More -ack Words

_____

_____

_____

_____

_____

_____

_____

_____

_____

What is the -ack word?

What Is the -ack Word?

quack!

ack

up

Mack has a pack
that he wears on his back.
It smacks and it whacks.
There's a lot in that sack!
There are books and a lunch
and a game and a snack.
and there could be a duck
cause we all heard a "___ack!"

**Put the puzzle together
to solve the riddle.**

Guess-Me Poems & Puzzles: Word Families Scholastic Professional Books

More -ail Words

_____

_____

_____

_____

_____

_____

_____

_____

_____

What Is the -ail Word?

_____

What is the -ail word?

e-m

ail

My grandma wrote letters
   she sent in the mail,
on birthdays and holidays.
   They came without fail.
But letters now seem
   as slow as a snail!
So grandma decided
   to send me e-__ail.

**Put the puzzle together
to solve the riddle.**

Guess-Me Poems & Puzzles: Word Families   Scholastic Professional Books

More -ake Words

_____

_____

_____

_____

_____

_____

_____

What Is the -ake Word?

What is the -ake word?

ake

Jake the snake
wanted to bake
something good
for his friend Drake.
They both live near a little lake
so Jake baked Drake
a soggy __ake.

Guess-Me Poems & Puzzles: Word Families   Scholastic Professional Books

More -an Words

_____

_____

_____

_____

_____

_____

_____

_____

What is the -an word?

What Is the -an Word?

Dan's father Stan
  is a very helpful man.
He drives on our field trips
  Whenever he can.
Six kids can fit
  in his super-size v____!

**Put the puzzle together
to solve the riddle.**

Guess-Me Poems & Puzzles: Word Families   Scholastic Professional Books

More -ank Words

_____
_____
_____
_____
_____
_____
_____
_____

¿What is the -ank word?

_____

What Is the -ank Word?

ank

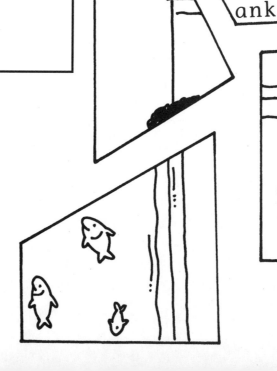

t

Hank's bright new coins
   go *clank, clank, clank.*
He's saving them up
   in his piggy bank.
Hank wants to buy
   a huge fish __ank.

**Put the puzzle together
to solve the riddle.**

Guess-Me Poems & Puzzles: Word Families   Scholastic Professional Books

More -ap Words

_____

_____

_____

_____

_____

_____

_____

_____

_____

What Is the -ap Word?

What is the -ap word?

snap

tap
clap

ap

yap

n

The squirrels yap.
   The chipmunks clap.
The turtles snap.
   The woodpeckers tap.
They wake the bear up
   from his __ap!

**Put the puzzle together
to solve the riddle.**

Guess-Me Poems & Puzzles: Word Families   Scholastic Professional Books

More -at Words

_____

_____

_____

_____

_____

_____

_____

_____

_____

What Is the -at Word?

What is the -at word?

at

Pat grabbed her hat
and her fat, wooden bat.
When her friends couldn't play,
Pat yelled out, "Drat!"
But then she hit balls
to her dog and her __at.

**Put the puzzle together
to solve the riddle.**

Guess-Me Poems & Puzzles: Word Families Scholastic Professional Books

More -ay Words

_____

_____

_____

_____

_____

_____

_____

_____

What is the -ay word?

What Is the -ay Word?

Whenever I'm sick,
  it's not a fun day.
But in certain ways
  it can be okay:
Mom and I have
  games we play,
and my meals come
  on a special ___ay.

**Put the puzzle together
to solve the riddle.**

Guess-Me Poems & Puzzles: Word Families   Scholastic Professional Books

More -eep Words

_____
_____
_____
_____
_____
_____
_____

What Is the -eep Word?

_____

What is the -eep word?

eep

From the mother bird's nest
    comes a "Cheep, cheep, cheep."
The babies are hungry,
    "Peep, Peep, peep."
The mother bird doesn't
    get much ___eep!

**Put the puzzle together
to solve the riddle.**

Guess-Me Poems & Puzzles: Word Families Scholastic Professional Books

More -ell Words

_____

_____

_____

_____

_____

_____

_____

_____

What Is the -ell Word?

What is the -ell word?

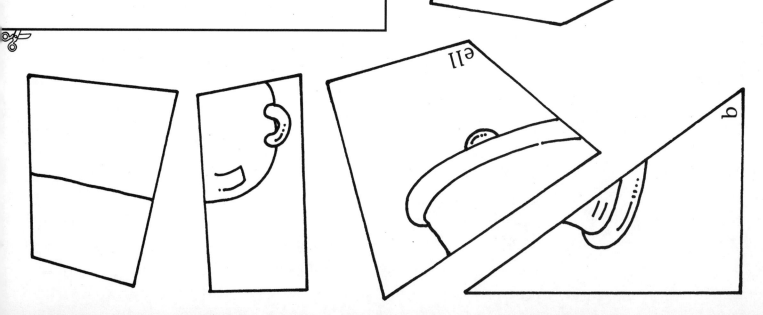

ell

b

When Nell brought Pup
   for show and tell
the day went
   very, very well.
The kids thought Pup
   was really swell.
He stayed in class
   till the very last __ell!

**Put the puzzle together
to solve the riddle.**

Guess-Me Poems & Puzzles: Word Families   Scholastic Professional Books

More -est Words

_____
_____
_____
_____
_____
_____
_____
_____

What Is the -est Word?

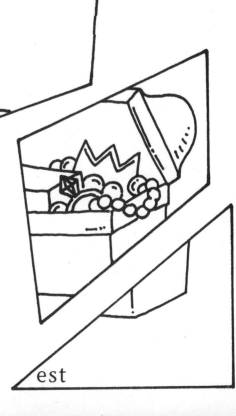

What is the -est- word?

ch

est

I found a map that had an X.

I dug and dug.

I did my best.

The whole day long I didn't rest

until I found the treasure ___est!

**Put the puzzle together
to solve the riddle.**

More -ice Words

_____

_____

_____

_____

_____

_____

_____

_____

_____

What Is the -ice Word?

What is the -ice word?

ice

Brice thinks pets are really nice

so he leaves out

bread, cheese, and rice.

But now he has

so many __ice!

Guess-Me Poems & Puzzles: Word Families   Scholastic Professional Books

More -ide Words

_____

_____

_____

_____

_____

_____

_____

_____

What Is the -ide Word?

_____

What is the -ide word?

is

ide

I just love water.
I kick and glide.
In the ocean there
are waves to ride.
But my favorite is
the water ___ide.

Guess-Me Poems & Puzzles: Word Families   Scholastic Professional Books

More -ill Words

_____

_____

_____

_____

_____

_____

_____

_____

_____

What Is the -ill Word?

What is the -ill word?

ill

h

One fine day,
 Jack played with Jill.
They had no pails
 that they could fill.
There was no water
 they could spill.
So they spent all day
 rolling down the __ill!

**Put the puzzle together
to solve the riddle.**

Guess-Me Poems & Puzzles: Word Families   Scholastic Professional Books

More -*in* Words

_____

_____

_____

_____

_____

_____

_____

_____

What Is the -*in* Word?

_____

What is the -*in* word?

in

gr

Many twins stick together
    through thick and thin.
Many twins have the same
    eyes, face, and chin.
Many twins seem to smile
    with the very same ___in.

**Put the puzzle together
to solve the riddle.**

Guess-Me Poems & Puzzles: Word Families Scholastic Professional Books

More -ine Words

_____
_____
_____
_____
_____
_____
_____
_____

_____
_____

What is the -ine word?

What Is the -ine Word?

If their dinner's not on time,
the swine all cry and whine.
But when the farmer comes
and it's finally time to dine,
they put on little bibs,
and stand in one straight ___ine!

Guess-Me Poems & Puzzles: Word Families   Scholastic Professional Books

More -ing Words

_____

_____

_____

_____

_____

_____

_____

_____

_____

What Is the -ing Word?

What is the -ing word?

ing

str

It's a spring thing

   when the birds take wing.

It's a spring thing

   to hear robins sing!

It's a spring thing

   to fly kites on a _____ing.

**Put the puzzle together
to solve the riddle.**

Guess-Me Poems & Puzzles: Word Families Scholastic Professional Books

More -ink Words

_____

_____

_____

_____

_____

_____

_____

_____

_____

What Is the -ink Word?

_____

What is the -ink word?

ink

dr

In summertime
we go to the sink
and make lemonade—
our favorite's pink.
We make a sign
with bright red ink
and sell everyone
a nice cold ___ink!

**Put the puzzle together
to solve the riddle.**

Guess-Me Poems & Puzzles: Word Families   Scholastic Professional Books

More -*ip* Words

_____

_____

_____

_____

_____

_____

_____

_____

What Is the -*ip* Word?

What is the -*ip* word?

ip

ch

When Kip went
on a sailing trip,
he brought cookies
and chips and dip.
What kind of cookies?
Chocolate ___ip!

More -ock Words

_____

_____

_____

_____

_____

_____

_____

_____

_____

What Is the -ock Word?

_____

What is the -ock word?

ock

r

Brock had lots of time.

The clock said 8 o'clock.

So when he got to school late,

Brock was pretty shocked.

For all that Brock had done

was walk down the block,

taking little baby steps

and kicking one small __ock.

**Put the puzzle together
to solve the riddle.**

Guess-Me Poems & Puzzles: Word Families   Scholastic Professional Books

More -op Words

_____
_____
_____
_____
_____
_____
_____
_____

_____

What is the -op word?

What is the -op word?

What Is the -op Word?

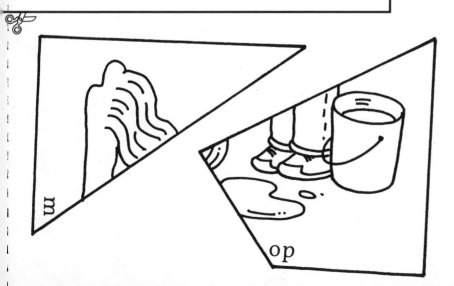

m

op

Mom said, "I'm so tired,
I'm just about to drop."
So I said, "You can stop, Mom.
I will cook and wash and shop.
And when the floor gets dirty,
I can clean it with the __op."

**Put the puzzle together
to solve the riddle.**

Guess-Me Poems & Puzzles: Word Families   Scholastic Professional Books

More -ot Words

_____
_____
_____
_____
_____
_____
_____

_____

What is the -ot word?

What Is the -ot Word?

ots

d

I bought some plants and seeds
for my vegetable garden plot.
I found a perfect spot
where the sun shone nice and hot.
Then to eat the garden pests,
I went out and I got lots
of pretty crimson ladybugs
with little black __ots.

Guess-Me Poems & Puzzles: Word Families Scholastic Professional Books

More *-uck* Words

_____

_____

_____

_____

_____

_____

_____

_____

_____

What Is the -uck Word?

What is the -uck word?

uck

tr

Chuck was having
  a little bad luck.
His wheels got stuck
  in the mud and muck!
His duck said, "Quack,"
  his chicken said, "Cluck,"
and they pushed the pickup
  right out of the muck.
Then they drove away
  in his little red ___uck!

Guess-Me Poems & Puzzles: Word Families   Scholastic Professional Books

More -ug Words

_____

_____

_____

_____

_____

_____

_____

_____

_____

What Is the -ug Word?

What is the -ug word?

I caught a firefly in my jar.
    It had a light you can't unplug.
It wasn't happy in the jar.
    It wasn't feeling very snug!
I let it go in the nighttime air.
    That pretty, little, flashing __ug!

**Put the puzzle together
to solve the riddle.**

Guess-Me Poems & Puzzles: Word Families Scholastic Professional Books

More -ump Words

_____

_____

_____

_____

_____

_____

_____

_____

_____

What Is the -ump Word?

What is the -ump word?

Today we went to
the garbage dump.
The dirt made the truck go
"bump, bump, bump."
We threw out leaves
and an old tree ___ump.

**Put the puzzle together
to solve the riddle.**

Guess-Me Poems & Puzzles: Word Families Scholastic Professional Books